Poems from the Big White Shed
Nottingham Poetry Festival 2024

Published in Great Britain in 2024
by Big White Shed, Morecambe, Lancashire
www.bigwhiteshed.co.uk
Printed and bound by Imprint Digital, Devon

ISBN 978-1-915021-29-8
Copyright © individual authors of the poems in this book
Cover Design by Robert Lever

A CIP catalogue record of this book is available
from the British Library.

CONTENTS

FOREWORD

In the run-up to Nottingham Poetry Festival 2024, Big White Shed opened their virtual doors to anyone who wanted to write poetry and have the opportunity to be published. For many of us, attending in-person writing workshops is difficult, so the Zoom meeting has been a great way of reaching out to include people.

During six online sessions, on different days, at different times, we met a wonderful mix of writers, from across the United Kingdom and beyond (as far afield as Western Australia). All participants, whether they attended all or some of the sessions, have been invited to submit poems to be included in this anthology of writing.

The poems in this book reflect the variety of poets who came together. We hope you enjoy them.

Huge thanks to Nottingham Poetry Festival for the opportunity to host these workshops with this marvellous group of writers. I have been so impressed by the writing we produced in those few hours. This book includes some of the poems written in the sessions alongside poetry written at other times.

Anne Holloway
Editor, Big White Shed

ANGELA McG

April Pantoum

I feel curious.
The egg-yolk-yellow and the purple floor cloths no longer
hold back the water.
April is the month of my birth.
Will people come to Scotland because it still rains here,
one day?

The egg-yolk-yellow and the purple floorcloths no longer
hold back the water.
I make room for the steady flow of sky's tears.
Will people come to Scotland because it still rains here,
one day?
I feel bored.

I make room for the steady flow of sky's tears.
The mist slopes down the half-shaved hill.
I feel loved.
Inside, the weather is complicated and changeable.

The mist slopes down the half-shaved hill.
April is the month of my birth.
Inside, the weather is complicated and changeable.
I feel curious.

Tanka(ish)

Oh to be a flower
emerging, green through brown,
replenished by warmth, rain,
and dog breath. Never
questioning her place
in the family of us.

DAVID HUNTER

Big Window Dream

Behind that big penthouse window
I live that pleasant married dream,
Wedded to the American Dream
Divorced from the reality below.
Hustling, heaving tiny ants,
Scurrying to serve big ants
Imprisoned in the anthills towering above.

Towers which sway and shift in strong breezes
Waving in greeting
To other prison towers
To people half- glimpsed through other big windows,
Strangers.
People half-remembered,
Left behind,
Abandoned,
Do they remember me?
Do they care?
Are they still there?

Living their own imprisoned dreams
Of freedom and affluence
Just out of reach.
Fantasies of freedom
Fine dining, fast cars
Getting a life
Down payment on fulfillment
Pay what's owing when you can,
Free to chase clouds of happiness.
Floating by the big window
Glinting in sunlight
Misting the glass
Hold fast while you can.

Rectory Stones

Hearth stone long cold
Like hands that laid it
Chimney blocked.
If stones spoke,
What would they say?

No welcoming blaze in due season.
Strangers wander as they will.
No sense of place,
Nor times remembered.
Storm, pageantry and pestilence,
Strife and suffering,
Pomp and pride.

Strangers knowing nothing,
Heavy of tread and shrill of voice,
Respecting little,
Caring still less.
Yesterday's nobility and family
A curiosity and a peep-show.
World and his wife tramp through without leave,
Then depart who knows where.

Propagation

Proper tools for the job
is what you need for the art of propagation.
Workmen (and women too) often blame their tools,
human nature is what it is
and just what you need is a matter for disputation.

Some say knife blades should be curved
others will have them straight.
Whichever you have they must be sharp;
tools for that, is a whole new ball game,
Welsh slate, lubricants, whirring wheels, nifty gizmos you
can hold or clamp to the bench,
(watch they don't fly off)
and blocks of carborundum.

There's loppers and saws,
billhooks in all shapes and sizes
alarming diagrams galore,
like medieval instruments of torture.

Propagating houses and domes,
floating mulches and cloches,
for all tastes and all classes,
fill the pages of catalogues in profusion.

There's sticky traps and spring traps,
revivers, inhibitors, copper tape, stimulators and wonder
sprays in plenty,
gloves and goggles and masks to protect you;
they all come in handy,
what's supposed to be good for plants
will not always benefit humans.

The question remains,
which none can explain,

is how plants managed to grow and evolve
for millions of years
without gadgets or humans to drive them.

It's one of life's great mysteries.

RICHERPRIORITY

A Question of Summer

Sunny days but cloudy doubts,
changing the angles of your wind.
Trees have never looked their best,
with all this clear illusion
I should put my sunglasses on but maybe a jacket.
The cloudy thoughts are breaching,
Let me take a fine second to fine tooth this moment,
wait is it really half seven this evening,
better close me curtains.

Cloudy doubts, ohhh cloudy thoughts.
Puddles are for jumping in,
so these wellies make the catch,
plus the fish I'm gunna be pulling in, phwwooaarr.
Hmm cloudy thoughts hmm
(mum's voice) *don't forget to take your coat,*

If I'm going down memory lane
I'm gunna need a 10 pence ice pole, ha ha inflation.
Usually, it's just a sheet of rain encased with,
The Rain in Spain Falls Mainly on the Plain.
Damn, cloudy thoughts again.
Now let's go and enjoy what's left, said the English man.

Life is in the Small Print

Life in the spectre of madness is full of chicken scratches and smoking patches, overgrown masses talking about fashion, fascist and plastic. Fuck it, buy the package, live a life of average, till they pull the cords so your average way to survive is unravished.

Life is full of contracts, mobile phones with contacts, no bag of tricks or fun facts just overrated rated Dereks in dumb hats, suitcases N glad rags, saved by the bell but still get suffocated by the bank's bag.

A Birdseye View

If pure amusement with clear illusion to fuse infusion, one simple solution, without disputing this dark commuting. With no fear or confusion, I'm here to prove that it's more than stupid it's tortured rooting that you're influencing. So, upon the youths and crowd secluding, without including immune seclusion, you need to re-tune your tuning. As this world keeps turning from the sun and the moon, I'll stay high above, getting that Birdseye view

JOSIE ADAM

Sturdy Boots

Sturdy boots, of course, that's a given.
Splashing through puddles of the April showers
Worth a hat of some sort, really
I'd wear a shawl, in weather like this.

Splashing through puddles of the April showers
I didn't bother with a coat for gardening
I'd wear a shawl, in weather like this.
New life in every direction

I didn't bother with a coat for gardening
Planted in memory for one lost far too soon
New life in every direction
The evening cools, but doesn't darken, not yet

Planted in memory one lost far too soon
But still the time of year remembers.
The evening cools, but doesn't darken, not yet
Sturdy boots, of course, that's a given.

The Trouble Is

The trouble is
Once you have one disability
They just seem to stack
"Oh, chronic pain? Don't worry, we throw in
Chronic fatigue
Absolutely free of charge"

The treatment for one worsens the other
The doctor for your joints says,
"You must exercise! Cardio! Strength training!"
The doctor for the fatigue says,
"Stop! For the love of god, Stop running! Stop climbing!
Never exercise again!"

(Then there's the rheumatologist
and the cardiologist
and the physio
and the geneticist)
I want to put them all in one room
Let them argue it out without me

Pacing is the key, they say
Not pacing around the room
(because that's too much exercise)
But taking breaks
Learning your limits
Balancing
Planning
Prioritising

Impetuous decisions are outlawed,
Impulsive choices forbidden,
Whims are right out.

The trouble is
The person who knows my body best is me
I have to project manage my health
Listen to all the experts
Take them under advisement

The trouble is
I don't want to

I used to be fine
I used to dance
I used to ride
I used to roadie
I used to hike and climb mountains
I used to compete for my country
I used to win

The trouble is
I don't want to project manage my health
I want to run, and jump, and dance
I want to carry my own stuff around
And go out on a whim
To walk through the woods
And not have to worry if I'll make it home

The trouble is
My hip is caning right now
(and the painkillers are... not)
My hands hurt too much to craft
But I can type
I can think

I still have my words
so you get my words.
They had better be enough
because most days nowadays
they're all I have.

Daughter of the Stage and Silver Screen
(With acknowledgement to Rattigan
and thanks to Becca Miles.)

A stranded generation
No big brothers to guide them through.
The spotlight is on them:
The ones who watched their fathers leave for war
And never come home.

The limelight gives the curtain a rosy glow.
A child in white tarlatan stands centre stage.
The house full of men in khaki grey
Their eyes full of pain and grief
Desperately seeking relief.

She dances.
The men smile.

The lone figure taps across the stage
Not as skilled as the chorus line
Who finished moments before:
She's a child after all.

But she shines;
She takes the light she's given
Reflects it back a thousandfold,
Fills their hearts as they yearn for the innocence of youth.
The days before they knew war, and pain, and grief.

No mud filled trenches here;
Yellow light and scarlet curtains and
Gold paste covering the walls.

The young girl grows,
She learns to sing -
Men still stare and smile.

She cannot fight to save her brothers
No patriotic march for her.
Yet she has her duty still
If she can spark even the slightest joy
That's the reward of duty done.

The war ends, and too few come home
Not just men - the nurses and the drivers
And the munitions girls - they too are lost to the horror
show.

She dances on.
The rhythm of her life the tap of her shoes
The three-piece band in the orchestra pit.
The applause that rolls through the house.

Can she make them smile?
Can she make them glad?
Can she do her duty?

The cameras come.
A different world,
Sterile
Fragmented
Silent.

Sets and scenes and shots,
Silver and grey and black and white.
No colour here, no sound.

Is she doing it right?
She can't see their smiles,
Can't see the faces
Of the audience waiting for her song.
Just the empty glass eye
Gazing sightless at her painted face.
The path is laid before her feet,

As it always has been,
Take a step and smile.
Do this, do that
Be witty, be pretty
Be charming and sweet.

A silver world lies ahead
(cold and sharp and bright)
A golden world behind
(warmth and light and love)

The spotlight's on her, waiting for her choice.
"Take a step forward," they say.
"Silver's the future
No value left in gold."

She can't make herself step forward
She's told she can't go back
And so instead

She dances.

HONGWEI BAO

Routine

In our daily, post-dinner walk,
you let out a pleasant cheer:
Someone's taking over that newsagent.
It's going to be a barbershop.
Another barbershop? I frown.
There's already three in this area.

We walk down the deserted high street,
A woman with silver hair staggers past.
I sniff the air: *She must smoke a lot.*
you nod: *I saw her smoking fags*
at the corner the other day
Asthmatic coughs from a distance.

We smile at the friendly Indian guy
with a small, black dog on the leash,
gently telling her to stop yelping.
We fumble in our pockets and then
apologise to the man sitting
at the entrance to Poundland.

The leaves are turning green,
and brown, and then gone.
Our gaits are getting slower,
hair saltier and pepperier,
words fewer in-between.

We walk on, day after day, following
the same road, remarking on the same
things – well, almost the same.

Confession

We kissed at the Mardi Gras last summer
under the rainbow-coloured Australian sun.

The cross necklace on your neck
dangled in front of your chest.

Now I see you
wake up each night, gazing

at the cross, tears in your eyes,
remorse on your face.

How can you
stagger into church on a Sunday

morning, hair messy, alcohol
on every breath, struggling

to stay still in a pew, nodding
sheepishly to the hypnotising

story of Adam and Eve, queuing
for a pathetic looking

piece of wafer and a drop
of sugar-loaded wine, after

a Saturday night out at a gay
club, drinking shots, dancing

till your legs are sore, laughing
till your heart aches?

And how can you
still pick up that black-bound,

stern-looking book and pray?
What have you told

the priest that you won't
share with me? Have I ever

featured in your heart-
wrenching confession?

Spring Thoughts

The air is crisp, the sunshine gentle, blue sky with
patches of white clouds.
Who'd compare their lover to a summer's day – what's
good about the summer?
In North China where I come from, summer is fiercely hot
and dry.
Spring is daffodils, tulips, cherry blossoms and dancing
bees.

Who'd compare their lover to a summer's day – what's
good about the summer?
Who says April is the cruellest month? It can be gentle
and mild.
Spring is daffodils, tulips, cherry blossoms and dancing
bees.
Wellingtons, jumpers, waterproof jackets will take you
anywhere into the wild.

Who says April is the cruellest month? It can be gentle
and mild.
Walking along the ancient city wall, feel the breeze
carrying the fragrance of spring.
Wellingtons, jumpers, waterproof jackets will take you
anywhere into the wild.
Standing on the steep hill, watch the waves washing the
shore.

Walking along the ancient city wall, feel the breeze
carrying the fragrance of spring.
From North China to North England, I take the memory of
you with me.
Standing on the steep hill, watch the waves washing the
shore.
The air is crisp, the sunshine gentle, blue sky with
patches of white clouds.

KATHLEEN LITHERLAND

In Weather

Out on the water, sun specks sparkling,
Gusts of wind catch me unexpectedly.
Feeling the sting of cold on my cheek.
Wind! Excitement!

Gusts of wind catch me unexpectedly,
A stinging that makes me feel alive.
Wind, excitement,
When I venture out.

A stinging that makes me feel alive.
What more do I need
When I venture out?
The gale blows beyond the walls.

What more do I need?
Alive and battling the wind,
The gale blows beyond the walls.
Out on the water, sun specks sparkling.

The Body

My lungs burn!
I gasp for air!
I feel my breath choked.
My oxygen reserves fall to critical levels.
My skin is feverish, over-heated, cracked, and dry.
I melt in a desperate attempt to cool.
My bones ache, I groan,
My skeleton is crushed and broken – turned on the rack.
I am ground to dust.
My arteries run with poisons
That are slowly destroying me.
My flesh is filled with rotting filth
That travels through my veins,
Infecting every part.

You are the torturer,
But I am not a victim.
I am slow to respond,
Yet once begun, I am a mammoth
That cannot be turned.

There will be a reckoning.

I will survive.

Will you?

What The Old Woman Said

All is well.
Everything is unfolding as it should.
The Darkness descends, the Wheel turns,
The Light returns,
All is well.

The Earth breathes in and out,
Listen to the heartbeat of Now;
Circles spiral through the seasons,
The stars spiral through the heavens.
Time is just the turning of the Wheel.
There is only the moment;

All is well.

JAKE DENNIS

The Summoning

For Stephanie
She saw Jacob... But she saw no one.
- Virginia Woolf (*Jacob's Room*).

Staring back at you, before he turns
into the maze, he hears your call then runs.
You follow—calling through the haze of growing
years—your peanut-coloured hungry boy,
sobbing in our silent room "Ja—cob!

Ja—cob!" Mrs Flanders' son returned
with half a jaw. Through countless paths of rerun
scenes of leafy search, your eyelids straining
shut to knot your present in, your boy
ahead. Your voice awakens me to touch

your furrowed face. Like a rabbit sprints
his features dart behind a corner. You chase
them round the labyrinth. Shaking through cypress,
                                             you cry

his name aloud, cling to sleep to keep
grief—morning's knives of light—out.

To stay in dreams of play each day you run
through the maze of yesterday he comes.

Symphony in G minor
For Steph

i
Eager players prick the tender air,
allegro con brio; an electrified pulse.
Each arpeggio flight an impulse predestined
by pen to descend through Mozart's 25th.
The symphony stops. Applause. The orchestra waits.
The curly haired conductor sniffs: the tempo
slackens to *andante,* like a dementia patient
waltzing in her private room. On cushioned
red velvet I draw my date to me.

ii
Fortepiano: the sudden pain that bludgeons
the brain renders a stranger ahead nearly
unable to mumble or shriek against the heat
of blood's increasing rush and light's ill-
timed vacation. The assault of colourless light
shimmers musicians' black threads to grey.
The stench of perfume and sweat sickens
as the glittering of varnished celli darkens and dims.
Spotlit by Wolfgang, the trio works for us.

When truly ill and adult, too polite
are we to explode our private hell on others.
Careful to protect the scene, we hold
our breath like thieves, stiff in shadow, crouching
from Order's searchlights. Foul fragrances betray us.
What heroes! We are sorrowful and sorry,
and sorry to vomit and shit, think ill-bred
to rouse family or strangers when streetlights are blurry
with frost but helplessly leave our wreckage of dust.
At gigs, where words are swallowed by whales of bass
and laptop beasts, a sudden surge of shoves

force the faint and drunk to the front; but here
where coughs and selfie clicks defile the soft
massaging solos of muted bassoons, we hear
a thud and thump from the third row below.
In Sziget, in clubs, the party rages on.
The conductor permits players stop this show.
My date looks to me to stay or go.

iii
Doctors filter down the aisle like rills.
Someone jokes "This: the most exciting
part." An older woman grabs binoculars.
Teachers direct their students out with ease.
"Someone call an..." I forgo a prayer.
St John's ivy green jumpsuits
arrive while nun-black ushers spot
then shoo the straying gawking twittering crowd.

We linger like school children told to look
away from *les enfants mechant*, a suicide
or porn, like kids who sneak back to watch
a car crash of curses from drunken uncles,
or an epileptic aunty wriggle a dance
at a family party. Solemn as a hospice nurse,
a collective *fermata* enfolds the remaining crowd:
a morgue-blue luminance emanates from third row.

A magnet or prophet, the torch searches for a following
beneath glove-widened eyes. Then arms
like the branches of palms, wave for a covering white
as snow to place on the body. The woman is lifted:
her right hand to forehead; winter's storm
and stress breaks. Elbow blocking the ceiling
of lights and eyes like Suskind's pigeon hanging
over the balcony, she's carried out stage right.

iv

My date's prayer answered: the pensioner
is cleared. We reclaim our seats. "What
an intermission!" *Improvvisato*
a lone flutist warms up on stage
con anima. Backstage, the conductor determines
to finish the fourth movement while one nurse
returns to calm then claim the patient's husband.
On my knee my date, a studying nurse,
rests her calming hand. Life's grand.

The Catch

For S. E. Dennis

Thumb-pricking threaded fetid prawn
plops in breezy noon's glittering ripples.
Like staring shag, the lad awaits in shade:
beneath his seat the ants maintain their route.

'round reeds and rigid roots the bream are drawn
through murky light toward the shrouded sickle.
Ants and chair upset, a trade is made:
a life for a bite. Jack reels in his fruit.

Eye to man and dirt; bleeding, stunned,
twitching, mutely mouthing, hook retrieved,
the silvery freed slippery bream's recaptured!
Eye to dusk and river, hungry fecund
hunters (bird, fish, and man aggrieved)
honour Nature's rule. Her ants regather.

KERRY McKEEVER

When We Are All One Community

He's finally stopped sulking today.
Universe is ignored when he bursts through
How loved he is
cement skies have been too clingy recently.

Universe is ignored when he bursts through
beaming yellow spotlight whispers to my ankles
cement skies have been too clingy recently
brown hair relieves my moist neck.

Beaming yellow spotlight whispers to my ankles
twitching curtains settle with a tea
brown hair relieves my moist neck.
It doesn't matter the toast got burnt.

Twitching curtains settle with a tea
undressing myself of the blue flowery scarf
it doesn't matter the toast got burnt
he's finally stopped sulking today.

Naïve Dull Night

Candlelight shivers
across smirking
university faces.
It's 1995.

We have been chanting
for 17 minutes
testing the bravery,
and stupidity, of each of us.

We place 10 finger tips
on the base of the glass, again,
and join our leader
as he calls upon spirits.

Fingers are whiplashed
chair legs screech. Words
stampede and everyone
owes the swear box money.

Our leader takes control
as though convincing
toddlers to stop
eating sweets.

We go again.
Fingers rattle, voices freeze
and promises collide.
Do you have a message?

My bottom lip starts bleeding
eyelids slam shut
hearts explode from chests.
The glass drags itself
and us from seating

to standing
whilst debating the invite
Yes!

We drain the room of oxygen
and nod
Who is it for?
Left, right, forwards, backwards

forwards, right, left
left, right
it stops in front of her.
We all forget to breathe.

I Don't Want to Ruin Your Good Day

If sewn lips could talk,
firstly they would tremble.
You'd watch her fight with the lump
wrapping around her vocal chords.

She'd widen her eyes to stop the escapees
and she would stare hard,
as if deciphering words
that hang in the air.

She would inhale so you could hear,
her stuttering breath
and your ears would detect
picking of broken fingernails

She'd scratch the skin on the
back of her hand until it wept
and then wipe
weeping blood into her other hand.

Her breathing would calm
she would find your eyes,
and give you a feigned laugh
It's fine, really, let's not talk about it

And then she would sew her lips
back together
because in her mind,
she doesn't want to burden you,

with her mind
she wants to forget,
it's just sometimes
the stitching comes loose.

MAYA O

My Coffee

In mornings I get up to make my coffee.
Of course, not just for that, but first, the coffee.
My black and hot, and bitter coffee.
I make it my, and grandma's way.
Just spoonful of coffee in my cup.
The ground one, not the instant one.
The pinch of cinnamon and few little cloves.
That's it, just add hot water, cover the cup, and wait.
The cup is not inherited, just the method.
I wish it was inherited, the cup.
It's not, just lookalike.
The cup is vintage and preloved,
And just reminds of grandma's one.
The coffee is the main, not the cup.
As dark as night, as bitter as a life
And hot as love.
Is my forever coffee,
And grandma's coffee,
What I love.

I Love Trees

I love trees.
They never preach,
They teach.
By their actions.
You can hug a tree
And it will never
Push you away.
It will give you, its strengths.
You can smell its blossoms,
Kiss its leaves,
Or eat its fruit.
The tree will never say no.

You can tell everything to a tree.
It will never judge you,
Or gossip about you,
Or tell you off.
You can lay under a tree,
It will give you a shade
And sing you a lullaby
Of whispering leaves.
With birds who nest there
Joining in.

I want to be buried
With a seed of a tree,
To grow in a tree,
To become everything
This tree is.
And to grow
In the next seed
Of that tree
And the next
And the next.
And to be all

That this tree is
Forever and ever.
I love trees.

A Poem a Day

Poem a day keeps doctor away!
Do I need to read it, or write, or perform?
Just choose the right option!
Or use all of them.
It's up to you always, what works just for you.
Or make your own option, your very own version.
You can write up a poem on a piece of the paper,
Make the paper airplane and fly it away.
It's just a suggestion, do what works for you!
Just remember, that poem a day keeps doctor away!
Always! That way!

BRIAN CLARKE

Leavef

Gently the leaf tumbles and falls,
floats, swirls and turns fast and slow
Along the path of the river
as though above,
rather than on top of the water
Negotiating the occasional wind
as would a feather.

Enchanted, I watch the leaf
deliver its solo performance.
With supremely skilful, graceful movements
Demonstrating a dance of a grace sublime,
Delivered for the first and the very last time.
In particular for no-one,
Though (if they are inclined) maybe anyone.

As a mayfly would flit and a butterfly fly,
Gliding with the long slow grace of an ice skater,
Then stopping and turning as tight and precise,
as would a prima ballerina.
So very, delicately, carefully passing by.
Captured in slow motion, but complete
Within no more than a moment of time.

An appetite insatiable.
With keen concentration and anticipation
Looking forward to what is ahead
around this or beyond the next bend
and to what shall come next.
Curiously manoeuvring to observe
Then dismiss any passing interest

Collecting wants and needs like pollen.
Occasionally, but not very often.
Each meeting only ever fleeting.
Flirting with the currents and the eddies,
declining each in turn to be its partner.
Twirls and curls then swirling, ducking, bobbing and
weaving,
before turning around and moving on
to wander and to tempt another.

That were once strangers
become no longer strangers
to then return once again as strangers.
In as quickly as you are able to say;
This today, becomes their yesterday.
No requirement or purpose for any lasting acquaintance.
Temporary being the length of time this leaf needs.

Nothing is obtained from disappointment
So little shall be retained from what has been seen
The burden of Baggage,
neither desirable or possible
As time can only ever move on
As it is with the leaf,
A situation shared between them as common

All in that brief time is now passed,
Any photograph taken as a reminder
has no point and no purpose.
The chance encounter granted
our privilege and the witness what was to be its first,
and the very last dance.

Unable to stand still
As Delay = Stay
Pause, but Stop never.
So it Dare not. Ever.

It does not and Cannot.
Stationary is only ever necessary
whenever to negotiate the next manoeuvre.

Is the water the river?
(One being static, the other is never)
We only pass this way once
As is the passing of time
Twice only ever possible,
If met further down the line.
Few are invited and fewer inclined.

The river flows along,
Then on to the sea.
Nothing more to say,
Its just how it is,
And how it's meant to be.
Did the leaf perform its dance
as a compliment for me.

So what of that feather?
Its coming, expected never.
Its staying, expected forever.
A chance encounter encountered.
But unfortunately taken for granted
It came, now has gone.
And as does nature
moved on.

Thats the nature of leaves,
They leave.
Or... leavef.

Sweet Dreams, Sweet Prince
for my grandson, and my father

a pile of clothes upon the chair
or on the bed,
resting from the trials and the tribulations
that this day they have had.
The end of yet another busy day
Having chased all of the dragons that he must slay.
Another battle and accord secured
by the man behind the shield and sword
our pint-sized superhero
Dave Quixote

Another day secure and mankind saved
so rest your eyes and gently bathe
in the warm and soft luxurious cream
of dreaming your wonderful and mysterious dreams.
This dreamy tune I gently strum,
and stroke your brow I softly hum
my Lullaby for
(my tiny little bit dotty)
Dave Quixote

A gentle stroke
to ease a fading scowl,
a hanky dabs to
calm your fevered
Slipping to sleepers brow.

So, Sleep my sweet prince,
for the nasties cannot get you now
Sssssssssssssssshh,
and let the troubles clear
and from your mind's eye rinse
Dream your Sweet Dreams,
Dream on, Sweet Prince.

GORDON B

A Valentine Verse

old age for some,
is all about pipes
and slippers

but for me,
it's more about thinking of you
running around,
in little more than
frilly knickers

PRATIBHA CASTLE

St. Jude of The Lost Cause

In the ambulance, I remember
how that time before
I pretended
this is little more
than the specs I'd lost one spring

when, dazed as the cat
who ate her kit,
I haunted the garden,
hoped to find them
by the yellow irises
encircling the pond,
in the compost bin

from which I'd spread
a comforter
of mulch
for the baby beetroot
swelling in the dark
like clotted blood,
their bruised leaves
having weathered
the rude tweaks
of sparrows.

Almost teatime at the hospital,
midwife Mary chirrups
it's a boy and you are resting on my belly,
your blue gaze unblinking
as though taking stock,
searing me to the core, then,
before she snips

the lardy cord still linking us,
that's when I know
St Jude has come up trumps.

Sugar

I imagined childhood
might be stripped away
like wall paper
mapped with fungi,
ripped off to reveal
plaster pristine
as an infant's chuckle.

Yet the day I tugged a corner
peeling by my bed, plaster
crumbled at my feet,
recalled a pack of Tate & Lyle,
fallen by the stove, open
like a shocked child's O,
sugar grains congealed
by vapour from a kettle
whistling to itself
above lascivious flames.

I imagined childhood
might be shed, easy
as a genasai snug
across a girlish chest,
kicked under the bed
with spider husks
and moth-snack socks,
belief in gods
who pay attention.

Childhood, seized in cells,
proved an ambered wasp,
bubble in Venetian glass
tempered by unwelcome counsel.

What might melt
this clotted heart?
Thrush-song
skeined in dawn, jasmine
moonlit at an open window,
god's eyelash streaming nimbus gold.

How Can You Miss What You've Never Known

You follow signs across the Downs.
A bush ablaze with blood berries
from a child's pricked hands.
Acorns in jester bonnets.
Incense of trampled thyme.
Adonis blue's flickering Morse. A linnet,
silenced.

A badger's corpse,
life having quit
on dawn-mist paws,
flops by the root-
knuckled track
in the gloaming
of two hazels,
trunks entwined.

Grasses stir, as if the badger
snuffles still for worms
and lacquer-back beetles,
its imaginary breath
a limbo of life
and release, faltering,
the way you
falter at an unfamiliar junction
over which of three paths
to follow, hazed
as to where each leads.

A red kite keens, lures
you down a chalky trail,
across dust-stubbled fields,
the way beyond shadowed
by capricious clouds
and a grassy curve, enchanting
as a sleeping child's smile.

KATE BURNS

Violins

My children are violins brought home from school...

They screech and squeal, wild and loud,
But in their cacophony, music is found.

Though they miss notes and their pitch can be dire,
They are my little violins that I love and admire.

I tune them with care, though not always right,
Together we muddle through the days and the nights.

People marvel at the melodies, how sweet and how cool,
But don't know the chaos of violins fresh from school.

The Desk

In the heart of the bustling community centre,
where laughter intermingles with the occasional clatter
of dropped pens, and the soft hum of conversation,
there sits a desk.

Scuff tells tales of creativity and companionship,
marked with the stories of users past, weathered by time.
On this desk lies a peculiar assortment of items,
out of place yet intertwined.

Nestled amongst the worn edges of colourful Lego bricks,
bearing grubby prints of countless hands,
rests a ball of soft turquoise wool.
Fibres whisper of warmth and comfort,
of craft groups knitting and chatting.

Perched beside the wool, as if guarding it with shade,
sits a solitary pink lady apple.
Its rosy skin gleams under the glare
of the overhead strip lights,
natural beauty amidst the man-made chaos.
Perhaps forgotten by its owner,
quiet dignity amidst the lively surroundings.

The Lego bricks, once vibrant and new,
now bear the marks of time and use,
a testament to joy.

The ball of wool, soft and inviting,
holds the promise of countless hours spent in quiet
companionship,
weaving stories and memories.

And the pink lady apple, ordinary yet significant,
reminds us of the simple pleasures found in the everyday,
a reminder to savour sweetness.

A tableau of unexpected harmony.
The desk a silent witness to the ebb and flow of life.
Children gather, their imaginations ignited.
Knitters and crafters huddle.

And a staff member pauses to admire the beauty of the
pink lady apple.
A moment of quiet amidst the chaos.

Sleep Creep Leap

In the soil of silence, I lay my roots,
A perennial in the garden of life,
Last year, a slumber beneath the boots,
While above, the world spun in strife.

Surgery's blade, a harsh winter's chill,
Forced dormancy upon my frame,
But in that stillness, I found the will,
To weather the storm, to rise again.

Like the perennial, I crept and stirred,
Beneath the surface, unseen, unknown,
Reflecting, growing, my spirit heard,
In the depths of solitude, I've grown.

Now, as the seasons turn once more,
I emerge, stronger, from the fray,
New role, new wings, my spirit soars,
In the light of a brighter day.

With clarity born from introspection's art,
I embrace the journey, the path ahead,
Creative fires ignite within my heart,
As I weave poetry into the threads.

No longer dormant, but vibrant, alive,
A perennial in bloom, I stand tall,
For every trial, every tear, did strive,
To nurture the seeds of wisdom's call.

So let the seasons change, let time unfurl,
For I am rooted, resilient, and free,
A testament to the strength of the soul,
Like a perennial, forever, I shall be.

RUTH SINGLETON

With Our Hands

i.   Colouring the blanks

Space, made real through boundaries she says
she doesn't like rugs
or standard lamps in calming shades
just needs walls a place to sit
and skylights to help the day slide in
cold and off-colour, wearing slipper socks.
With our hands we make space she reaches up
above his head sees emptiness
ready to be adorned *with our hands we enclose*
they drag in a sofa
yellow as meadows
hammer tacks into the walls and hang
their history of prints cuttings holiday snaps.
The rest moves in – a deluge
of fiction on oak shelves
a pot plant leaves drooping. A long black cat
who will persist in nooks and on laps in this
place of smell and texture.
Old plans transposed on new maps he says
we can start to breathe here with hands
in pockets like he's fishing around for scraps of
aspiration.

ii.   Flickers in the rafters

Of course they find the place already warm
with goblin breath and ghost webs
slick and dripping on the insides of window panes
each morning. But how? She wipes and

wipes but ends in tears
the creatures echo in the rafters in the corners
of her ears. She had longed to be the first-heat
find an unsaturated space to belong
and to create
but the creatures must have got inside
their bags and boxes.
No he says *they were always already*
and inside the clicks of her knuckles and the ache of her
shoulders
she knows this is something
they can agree.

iii.   **Living with monsters**

She dabs condensation folds
time into a damp palm
clears her throat. The echoes ebb.
He begins to clean more talk more write
his body large against his new background
a monstrous imposition on small space
she thinks. She tends
ancestors of the potted ferns they bought in bright youth.
It's all wrong she taps a cigarette. Leaves leftovers out
for the night-time beasts that butt up against her walls
finds her father's face in a deep rainwater puddle
in the courtyard
in watermark stains on the heavy stone walls.
Wonders if peace can only be found at the far end of a
long taproot.
She rests a hand against the cool corner
of a table and tries to recall the shape
of home where she left it
whether it blossomed or fell.
He flicks the light switch and leaves.

My Keeper

I dream of keeping bees.
Not the reality of smoke and stings and sterilised jars,
But the thrumming life of it all.
The other-worldly chaos it foretells.
I dream of keeping chickens, also
the battery farmed ones
and have them sit on my shoulder
as we tour the garden's best scratching spots.
I kept two hamsters when I was a child,
unsuccessfully.
For now I keep a black cat. We fall out
and into love like sedimenting tidal pools
as the years drift.

SARAH WHEATLEY

The Fifth Season

and   I find you in the blue,
in the woods, and in the grain.

fleetingly   in sun-kissed motes
where fractured echoes hope.

clamouring in an afterimage.
grasping, flickering in my mind.

beauty   inherited through faces.
enduring beyond touch.

now in the blue, there is only silence.
my hands, empty since you let go.

I am lost within all this, our dreams long gone.
Before I could hide them away.

stillness addresses me,
and this day will soon be over.

outside, shallow snowfall thaws,
and spring attends renewal

STEPHANIE DENNIS

Book Store

Books a many
have you any?
The classical ones are best.

I came to the store,
to buy some more
and came home with a quest.

I read them all,
they piled up tall
and passed my literary test.

Cuddles of Love

Television, snacking, and sleeping
is super fun to do.
You never have to think,
you only have to chew.

Night and day we're hibernating;
it's too cold to blink.
So were wrapped up under the covers,
the sun is way too bright.

The fire logs still burning,
but so are our eyes.
The clock keeps turning and turning,
Goodnight, goodnight, goodnight!

Smokey Love
> for my husband Jake

My milk chocolate man,
you excite me when our lips touch.
Our bodies entwine between silk
under the twinkling stars.

Your warm hands surging over my body,
erecting my nip-ples.
Smoke from your cigarette buz-zed
my brain with its sex-ssence.

Vapours lifted past us into the sky,
forming heart shaped clouds.
This is our hot erotic love
floating into the air.

I suck on that peachy shisha,
going deeper into the garden of wonder.
A few blows float in the hot tub like
steam shooting out of the water.

JACK ROSCOE

These Distracted Times

I
Charles is back, not from the dead
For this one still has his head
But from history's trod.
He's happy at last
To break the cast
He'd spent a life imprisoned within.
With rhyme and some reason he'll rule
To avert the crime of high treason
That truncated his namesake.

Alas the shadow of Elizabeth
Might plague yet another Charles.
For in outer shires, the wires sing with #chat
That's he's #notmyking
Four centuries since a republic last stood
The young are asking if a
Sole bloodline_____
Should define how a nation's run.
This talk will shock and stun
The ones who thought the Royals won
The last world war.
Without the Crown, the lion's mane, scalped
And its roar mutes to mews, they say,
Look at history.

So we do and see
That when our nation trumped its king
Full triumphant it sang
And set on track a new England...

II

But we are trapped
By lives that oft lack
Imagination,
What Blake would call
Our mind-forg'd manacles.

These have augmented once again.
You see it writ in misery and pain
On the hopes parched by lack of rain.
You hear in the wails of babes
Whose hunger and cries shade
And derail our 'Great' charade.
You stink in the fetid sludge
From profits and grabs ill-judged,
A green and pleasant land decayed
By royal patronage betrayed.
The Crown Estate given to pound;
What hope will come from profit
If waters can only filth deposit?
And if you try assert the feudal right
Don't be aghast when folk respond with might.

III

These times distracted,
By leaden sins on our people enacted
From golden malls and vintage balls
Vast grievances emerge
That our futures diverge
In revolution once again.
A nation's pain
Rewinds and overthrows
The binds that strangle.
No more, we cry
And with it our ails die.
Know from past that people stricken by wanton griefs
Will only assuage or suffice as fates' beliefs.

STEVEN CORBETT

The 50p Sideboard

The 50p sideboard
sits starchily in the hall.
Best bargain ever.
Sleek, elegant.
Wood more in effect than reality.
Formica? Veneer?
Peeling in places
but with a dogged glamour
inlaid plastic handles
green baize draws.
A place once for
Sweet sherry, Babycham
the *best* cutlery
glasses used only on occasion.
Anyone for advocaat?
Now mostly the miscellaneous.
Blunt pencils, inkless pens
an incomplete pack of playing cards.
A postcard from Lanzarote
ticket stubs, a passport photo.
Things that linger.
Yet to be ascribed,
artefact or trash?

The Taste of It All

Sometimes I am 1979.
A malevolent pressure cooker
A steam drenched kitchen.
Tuesday's weekly reveal:
Sodden cabbage, rusty pork chops.

Sometimes I am 1993.
Dry tongued, and thirsty
A bass note throbbing in my chest.
Sucking the sweaty juices
From a tepid kebab.

Sometimes I am 1999.
A blanket in the park
Olives, French bread, white wine.
She sits shoeless in the sunshine
While I am the most sophisticated man that has ever
lived.

Sometimes I am 2010.
Waiting for words to emerge
From rhythmic rasping breaths
Dropping beads of water on to
Cracked and pale lips.

And sometimes I am 2020.
Asking her, telling her, begging her
To please drink the glass of f—ing milk

These Are the Boots

These are the boots that made the journey
That scaled the heights and trudged the depths
Made of mud and frost and dew.
Boots that walked with many, yet followed few

Boots of occasional wrong turns and missteps
Of summits, sunrises and sunsets
Of journey's, plans, adventures, friends,
Boots of beginnings and of ends.

But let me tell you of their best walk.
The unforgettable one, with the best view
Let me tell you again
Of how these boots brought me to you.

UMBILICA

Tempering

Clanging from bed, her movements
ring the grey morning thin.
Melt my metallic greetings, so our love
may be long, rod-like,
armoured from the cold.

VICTORIA ZOE CALLUS

An Embroidery Kit List

Embroidery starts with my parents' hands
Where they merge to unfold into my own

It is a task we started long ago:
The slow thread of rhizome
deep tangle of home

Perhaps this is why it requires
Thick skin and bright light

    An orchid that takes months to bloom.

Blue Hour

Reaching June it stretches
shifts from hidden seconds to
twenty-two spindled minutes

It pools in pissed on corners
crawls up crusted tiling
round gutters
down roofs

It pads the clouds with something
softer: than milk froth, cats' fur,
your
skin

and then bolts.

Birthday Cottage

Some days I pad through mist-rain, slow
Forget that ghost we call time and how
it has devoured everyone I love

Softly tread through mud
waiting for boots to stick
and when they do: go barefoot
allow the soft of my feet to pierce
over pebbles, sharp twigs
climb the wall like a cat; wait
for   the whistle of birds
          the howl of old foxes
          the flash of a storm

on return
you wrap me in towelling
we warm by (electric) fire
remember how good it can be to have skin.

ZO COPELAND

@zocowrites

Sunrise

After a long winter of 90 nights
Overhead white clouds float by
Finally shedding the weight of woollen layers outside
Bright sun beams down into squinted eyes

Overhead white clouds float by
Skinny denim clings to clammy skin
Bright sun beams down into squinted eyes
Flesh beneath begs to be exposed again

Skinny denim clings to clammy skin
Bare limbs ready beneath, waiting
Flesh beneath begs to be exposed again
The final unveiling

Bare limbs ready beneath, waiting
A seat at nature's fireside
The final unveiling
After a long winter of 90 nights

She Will But Roar

She cannot speak
She hasn't the words
We will never hear her talk
Or shout
We can harm her
Over and over
And she will make no sound
But oh, she will roar
Stamping her feet
Until our foundations shake
Spitting out at us until we're flooded
Narrowing her fiery eye
Until sparks fly
And we will take no notice
Of her song and dance
Her show and tell
Her elemental drama
Because she does not speak our language
And she will make no sound
But oh, will she roar
Shaking herself until the cracks appear
Shedding tears until we start to drown
Spitting sparks until we set alight
And we will listen with one ear
The other tuned to podcasts and politics
For she inconveniences us
But she cannot speak
She will roar
Roar in our deaf ear
As we look to terabytes and Teslas
She will tremble and cry
And set us alight
Finally speaking our language
As her soil fails our crops
Her fires take our homes

And her tides rise above us
In our slow descent into the depths
We will realise
She has been speaking all along
We didn't listen
And now we're gone

First Date

We met at the beach that day
All nervous giggles and edited life stories
Eeking out the day, slow moving moments
Pulled together like magnets
Even the ice cream man thought that we were sisters
Oblivious at the time
Sand in our shoes, wind in our hair
Salt on our hands from the pebbles
Impromptu pencils
Carving our names on this transient ground
As though we could transcend time
Repeating these hours eternally
With every ebb of the tide
As though life wouldn't continue
Filling in the missing pieces
As though truth wouldn't out
Staring out to sea from the shallows
Your arms scooped around my waist
And you kissed me like the sea laps the shore
Losing myself in the current of you
I opened up like an oyster
You drew a circle around us in the sand with your foot
As if you could protect us both from your past

SONIA BURNS

Tunnel

The photo is a shot within a dark tunnel, you at the back, taking the photo, P in front of you to the right, identifiable by his red hood, S and I far ahead in the middle of the tunnel, walking together. The photo is silvery apart from the red hood, we are just silhouettes in the distance. The tunnel is artificially lit from within and curves round to the left. There are a series of lights at the top of the tunnel – a repetitive pattern – but the mouth of the tunnel is hidden, there is no light at the end of the tunnel and we walk on in the darkness, small figures separated from one another. I think it is one of the tunnels on the Monsal Trail but I can't be certain, I was never sure why you framed this photo of a tunnel and gave it to us. The picture has a sinister quality, I can't even be sure who the figures are, if they were ever really us. The photo has lost all context, you and S broke up not long after it was taken and so much has happened since then. You got married recently and at the wedding I spoke to your mother for a long time and we talked about S who I still see occasionally. P and I are still together but it can be hard and sometimes I fear for the future and it feels like I'm walking down a long dark tunnel made of very tiny, grimy bricks and artificially lit, like a TV homicide and we are all facing away from the camera, no eye contact, no facial expressions, just shapes moving forward in the dark.

KEVIN JACKSON

Borrowed Light

Automatic Friday,
manboy hard up
against vending machine.

Smacked it,
shook it or tried.
And again.

Nothing came out
though its offers flinch
like loved gold.

Seemed like
all he had.
My sweet crushed angel

is footsteps
through the dim and glare,
all of it guilty.

Eyes of Water

Did you ever see
the moment
a leaf falls from
the tree?

These scraps
of love
they'll never
be enough

and lads like Cal
will drop alone.
Till we can meet
the whole dark-
ness entire
and behold stars.

Fear and Faith

Afterwards it seemed a dream.
A song returned to its silent
upbeat, entire and nearly perfect

Each hesitation presents
with savage frankness, more choices.

Darkness prickly where
it meets hair.

We approach along a tight-
rope, face focuses face,
balances, almost.

I was young, the height
of youth and wanted this
too much to make
a first move.

Between us a louder darkness.
This night has cancelled
the moon. We are the moon.
All love is a coming
to terms with god.

Afterwards it seemed a dream.
A song, entire, so nearly
perfect, returned
to its silent upbeat.
An ant found
drowned in a rose.

COURTNEY WARD

Sky Full of Stars

In a sky full of stars,
An expression of life.
A time of the day where
I can just howl into the night.
And give you a piece of my heart,
All over again.

In this night and in this hour,
We call upon the ancient power.
So desperately want to cry out,
But we know its alright.
Angels were meant to fly,
Just like you eventually did.

Colours in the sky shine super bright,
Its just you and I, you and I.
It's the time of night,
We were just wondering around, for the last time.
The memory of being here with you,
One I'll carry for the rest of my life.

In this time, in this place,
We are standing in our light that wont fade.
A bond so strong it wont break,
Where we can fly as butterflies,
Swim likes dolphins,
And run into the Greenland like tigers.

As every breathe continues on.
I only pray that your okay in the clouds above.
Come back to me, eventually.
Where we can rule the world, together.
On another starry night, like this.

Human

Unlearning the masking,
learning about me.
Once a loss of identity,
whilst trying to fit in.

Trapped in a cage,
from a bait that upset my stomach.
Needed help,
but forced to keep quiet.

Blaming me, hating me,
wanting to change to be like you.
I don't know who I am.
I am lost and afraid.

Crying out loud
but being told to shut the fuck up.
Had to hide it all away,
as my only option to survive.

'celebrating diverse differences', they say.
Earth embraces us, society don't.
Fighting against a broken system,
that doesn't like change at all.

I felt obliged once,
to accept my broken, masked life.
But I couldn't keep up appearances,
I couldn't keep lying to the world.

I am so much more,
than your fake reality.
I am breaking free of those systems, to be myself,
without societal consequences.

I am starting to like myself,
I see weirdness as uniqueness.
I have now realised I ain't crazy.
I am human too.

Big White Shed is an independent publishing house set up by Anne Holloway to offer a platform to emerging writers. Our model of publishing is particularly suitable for poetry.

Anne was one of the co-directors of Nottingham based Mouthy Poets young peoples' collective, and was Creative Director of Nottingham Poetry Festival in 2021/22. She runs a variety of workshops and events in person and online. She is Creative Lead on a project called Surviving by Storytelling at the Institute of Mental Health at University of Nottingham, exploring how writing poetry can support our mental health.

If you are interested in learning about the work we do, you can find more information on the website and social media.

www.bigwhiteshed.co.uk
www.anneholloway.co.uk

Instagram: @bigwhiteshed @webepoets
Facebook: @bigwhiteshed @annethepoet

Anne also runs an online poetry community: PoEmpower
https://poempower.mn.co/